More praise for Waco Porter:

"These poems explore life in detailed images both beautiful and disturbing. The sun shines like truth. So hard at times one must shield their eyes from glare to see the full depth of field, finely focused. These poems are grounded and embody the sensual. Vibrant beauty like black bodies in lavender dresses or seeing Kenya in the Kansas plains. Modes of travel, or at times, escape, vary from skateboards to horses. *Bus Stop* is where the village, the whole community of families, past and present, whether together or separated, lost or redeemed in love, meet; gather in order to depart, disperse to their lives where Waco captures their spirits individually and collectively, all striving for home, for love, and for a world that makes sense."

-Guy Reed, *Second Innocence* (Luchador Press)

More praise for Waco Porter:

"In *Bus Stop,* Waco Porter delivers a lyrical and rhythmic collection of poems that explore family, community, and the author's own experience in a world seemingly overcome with racism, both subtle and overt. These poems bristle with musicality while delving into issues of class and race in a post-industrial landscape of unchecked avarice where the American Dream is never fully realized. There are moments of great beauty, images of sorrow and suffering, but underneath all of it the grit and impetus to keep getting up."

-Shawn Pavey, *Survival Tips for the Pending Apocalypse* (Spartan Press)

Bus Stop

Poems by Waco Porter

Kansas City   Spartan Press   Missouri

Spartan Press
Kansas City, MO
spartanpresskc.com

Copyright © Waco Porter, 2020
First Edition1 3 5 7 9 10 8 6 4 2
ISBN: 978-1-952411-08-3
LCCN: 2020936504

Cover and title page image: Jon Lee Grafton
Author photo: Terrance Williams
All rights reserved. No part of this publication may be reproduced or transmitted in any form or by any means, electronic or mechanical, including photocopying, recording or by info retrieval system, without prior written permission from the author.

Acknowledgments:

Special thanks to Jump Start Arts Kansas City, Spartan Press

TABLE OF CONTENTS

Motivation and Consultation – My Father / 1
Black Skater / 3
Lavender / 6
My Carolina / 8
Bus Stop / 10
12th and Grand / 12
Middle Passage / 14
Cotton / 15
Maria 'n' Me / 17
Balance / 18
City by the Sea / 21
Debbie / 24
I Lay Dying / 27
Jesus is Homeless / 29
War Dogs / 31
Abridged Kids / 33
Dead Hair and Rolling Baskets / 34
Raggedy Jan / 36
Kansas / 37
Blackness / 38
The Chosen / 39
The Kennel / 40
What We Do When No One's Watching / 41
Wayco / 42
Maestro / 43
Above All Else / 44
ABCs of Life / 45

Flint Am I / 46

Dress Shopping / 47

What We Deserve / 48

Haircuts and Cold Drinks / 49`

The Village / 50

Issue / 52

If We Are Loving / 54

Work / 55

Dumpster Diving / 56

Strange Hands That Pray / 57

Sermon / 58

Penthouse / 60

No One / 61

Parking Lots / 62

Hospice / 63

Gray Matter / 64

Night Run / 65

175th / 66

B.P.s / 68

Escape Route / 69

Inner Peace / 71

Letter to 1985 from 2012 / 72

Mare Internum / 74

My World / 76

Olathe Riders / 78

One Love / 80

Paradise / 82

Tank Tops and Collarbones / 83

When you can't create, you can work.

- Henry Miller

This book is dedicated to parents, sisters, wife, babies, family, friends; coffee shops, roads, little notebooks, pancakes and pens!

Motivation and Consultation – My Father

Somehow we have to mythologize our fathers
        Turn them into heroes donning capes
        Carrying superfluous weapons
        Being omniscient omnipresent figures for
        us
        our sisters
        mother
        or anyone in need of rescue at a desperate
        hour
I don't deny those things, but what do I know
I know my father
        I've seen him charge into the night to
        protect a daughter with only a stick in
        hand
        Grit his teeth to get his point across
        Make my mother blush still after 50 years,
        Embrace my wife
        Pick me up off the floor in my weakest
        moment,
        And put me down to define boundaries in
        his house.
I don't deny those things, but why not romanticize
the image
        Deserving of its own currency formed
        from platinum
        Unable to be tarnished or counterfeited
        A genuine article if you will
        But what do I know

I know the stance,
    The laughter,
    The promises,
    Memories we disagree on,
    Talks,
    The right index finger pointing towards   the
finish line for awkward teenagers and grown men who
    might not have won
    this one
    but need to finish the race

Black Skater

I'm a skater
        Pushing down streets that gnaw on the soles
of my shoes
        Trip me up
        And swallow my skin and hair
The price of not paying attention or being caught off
guard
Or just being
        But I push
Right foot forward
I'm goofy
Perfect for these streets
These streets that turn little girls into mothers too soon
Walking 4 or 5 other kids to the store where they share
1 bag of chips
1 drink
But everyone gets some and no one thinks the grown-ups
are watching
        I roll off the curb
        Push
Lean back and let my wheels scream at old men on these
streets
They were young boys once, who weren't prepared for the
hustle of life and death
They barely make it to the corner,
Beg for change
And ask God to bless you
They were young boys who thought they could
outrun the fatality of poor planning

I stop and drop change into my future palm
Hear a verse from Proverbs or Psalms
  And push on
I pop an ollie over a manhole cover
  Push
  And push harder
It's hard work to get the wind to blow through nappy hair
The girls at the bus stop dance when it's chilly
Hair wrapped
Thighs getting thicker
Their babies suck on potato chips and listen to mommy argue with the invisible man who calls once a week just to piss mommy off
  I push
Crouch down to wave and peek into the stroller
  Then push past
Cruise downhill
Grown women trek these hills with grocery bags
Afros and gold teeth
Grey sweatpants and dirty flip flops
All their friends are life long
So their stories are old and fresh
They are Prospect and Troost with new paint
Each smile and wave is a memory shared
  I push
Pop up a curb
  Push toward another bus stop
Young men test my navigation skills
Moving out of sync with each other
Their heads entombed with music
Nonchalance
Focus

Desire
Contemplation
Hunger
Thirst
Something other than me
But I have to move
Leaning forward and back
Relaxing my knees
Narrowing my eyes
Giving each gladiator his earned space
Praying he doesn't have black lips or burnt fingertips or a prune shaped liver
These are the survivors that hurdle obstacles and lean in to knock down walls
I earn a head nod and two fingers up
My wheels glide over cracks
    And I push
Another church
Another cop, car lot, and hair shop
    I push
Hands on my naps
Cramps creeping into my calves
I see my mother's face in a window
If God is as good as she says
Girls will grow slowly
Young men will survive and prosper
Old men and women will keep memories, friends and pennies
    I push
Right foot forward
I'm goofy
Perfect for these streets

Lavender

Black girls in lavender sundresses have gardens and children
These black girls also have good men
These men kneel and push their newborn sons and
daughters fingers into the soil
    Digging
    Turning
    Planting roses
He only stands to prune trees that provide unnecessary shade
The kneeling man talks to his children about the
importance of sunlight and water for things to grow
He checks the garden with his family often
    Pulling weeds
Describing the scent of roses
When his daughter pricks her finger on a thorn
He kisses the pain, lets her run to her mother
But warns his children that beautiful things have to
protect themselves from curious invasions
He always works on his knees in the garden
Close to the soil
Eye level to his children
In arms reach of black girls in lavender sundresses
He is close enough to the soil that subtle breezes form dust
clouds he inhales with delight
He is eye level to his children so he can speak and teach
and touch and listen without effort
He is in arms reach of black girls in lavender sundresses
A woman he knows by the impression of her feet in the soil
The braids that dance in Autumn winds
The palms that wipe his forehead

On this day

He stops his work

Turns his body and lays on his back for a moment

He asks anybody if this is what Eden should have been

He watches the sundress fly away

He hears the faint thud of diapers hitting the ground and the giggles of innocence

He feels a tug at his trousers

      The wind stirs

He smells the roses

And tastes soil

My Carolina

Pebbled driveways
Live oak limbs bowing under the weight of Spanish moss
which caresses the Carolina lawn
My fourth grade class is shuffling around the mansion
looking at parlors and drawing rooms wooden staircases
and empty kitchens
>	I see secret passages and holes in the walls
>	and banister
>	I look around and I hear footsteps that are
>	not ours
>	I hear orders spoken
>	pots clanking
>	feet running up and down the stairs
>	cards shuffling
>	ice rattling into glasses

My class sees the leather saddles and homemade tools
>	I hear singing and grunting outside
>	I hear shrill whistling, horses struggling under
>	the weight of the wagon
>	I hear a baby's cries muffled by the sweat on its
>	mother's back
>	I smell biscuits and bacon and sweat and smoke

My class sees the ornate gardens and flower baskets
>	I hear cannons and screams
>	I see musket balls implanting themselves into the
>	walls and banister
>	I look at Ms. Willis talking to my class

I look up and see the chandelier shaking
I feel plaster from the ceiling falling onto my face
I hear panting and a pistol cocking beneath
the floor boards
I look into the broken mirror in the hallway and
see black bodies disappearing into the walls and
floors behind me
I look at my class

We are light years from tribal politics
European ships
Bibles and whips
Written documents from abolitionists

But these images are in my lips
My sister's faces
My mother's cooking
My father's need to keep us all together
My grandmother's choices
My grandfather's eyes
Granny's smile
Gramp's toothpicks and money
    I hear Ms. Willis calling for me to keep up
    with the class
    I tell her my mother's grandfather is waiting for
    me at the river
And I run

Bus Stop

To man each his own voice
    On streets foul with confusion and resistance
In pulpits scattered with money and lost souls
    In my head with the doubt and disturbance
To each his own voice to argue with passion or dismiss with aggression
    I choose the voice of the street preacher
    I'll listen and take lessons in passion from the veins throbbing in the forearm and the side of the neck
Hands hardened from day jobs, unfiltered cigarettes and an old life
The uncombed mane that shows the focus on another part
The lion heart
The oversized social action t-shirt covering as much dirt as it can on the sweatpants that mirror the worn out Jordans
But Mike didn't do this work
He didn't carry his bible with its yellowing pages and crumbling spine and fading family tree
    He didn't speak about bondage and passages and self-awareness
He stopped, popped and dropped
And he flew
And he won
And we admire
    But the preacher's study
    And stand
    And speak
    And we question

Cause their shots seem so far off we can't tell whose won or lost
So they don't gain our admiration
They get our angst and disdain
Cause it hurts to listen and be close to smelling history seep out of sweat glands, nappy hair and saliva spilling truths
      The streets are alive with promise
Stop
Pop
And drop
And fly
Or
Study and speak and reach for something higher
than the rim
I admire them

12th and Grand

Alone
Palsied
With a cane, head wrap and fresh make up
Bailing grandsons out of jail constantly
Listening to lies and promises intertwine with her own desire to go back home
> Back to working men and baby making
> Back to porches in the summer and wood burning stoves in the winter
> Back to talking to boys and keeping both feet on the floor like mama said
> Back to her father's carriage and her mother's heavy hands
> Back to the river where she played, and bathed, and got baptized
> Back to her grandmothers arms if she could run fast enough
> Away from the addicts and smells and smoke and traffic

These streets aren't home
At home her neighbors we just as loud and the kids were worse, but she could call them all by name and tell them to shut up
At home food or a good fist fight seemed to solve any problem
> At home everyone was poor

At home marriage was a requirement and children were needed
At home you worked or went to school, but everybody went to church on Sunday

At home the police were just as bad, but she changed
their diapers, slept with their fathers and bullied their mothers
in grade school
At home there were chores and crowded spaces, but
everyone was loved and holidays were special
At home her mother sang at church and gossiped, her
father drank and played cards
At home her grandson would work in the fields like
her brothers and would be too tired to get into trouble,
At home her daughter would still be young and pregnant
and scared like her
        But at least she'd be home

Middle Passage

When I think of slavery
        I think about being made to believe my body
is not my own
        It belongs to the highest bidder
        And works when and where commanded
I look around and see lands I am not from
My family far from my sight
        My eyes and hands open and close while I work
I feel sweat inching down the crevice of my back, down
my chest and arms, through my hair and into my eyes
        My veins pulsing
        My skin breathing with power
The work of a slave is difficult but I am strong
        My teeth clench so tight my jaw clicks
        A howl surges from my belly
        My knees raw
        My mistress pleased

Cotton

Hands under shirt under bra
        Panties on the floor
I think we've done it all until you yell out a name
I don't recall
        I fall back into you hard
My knees clamp and trap your hand
        You choke on my hair and grab my neck
        Forcing me to stand and turn around
I feel a hand in my back
        A pillow catches my face
The pillow stinks
        Panties still on the floor
Toes curling under my feet
        I bite the pillow wet from saliva
You pull my hair
        I fight the urge to give in
The pillow taste good
        I remember why
It taste like yesterday
        It was a wild horse and you taught me how to break it
What to do with my hands
        How hard to buck and take control
Don't be afraid
        This apartment's full of wild horses you said
        And it takes a strong back and thighs to break them
I told you I'm up for the task

Then I asked
      What do you know about breaking wild horses?
I felt a sting a shockwave surged through my body
      You said the safe word is cotton

Maria 'n' Me

I'm obsessed with sex and death
    Lay me out on the linoleum baby til I got nothing left
Mixing blood and semen
    My passion in the pipeline
Saturating the sewer
    Floor drains contain my lifeline
Your paws emit claws
    Fangs sprang from your jaws
Howling for your savior
    A sacrifice for your God
Entomb me in wombs
    While Herod strikes the young
Share this with the shepherds
    One dies
One comes

Balance

Another day and time
You wouldn't know about documented and undocumented workers
You hire working men with families
You will die in your grandfather's house
Your wife will find you at the bottom of the stairs with cash and bills in one hand, wallet in the other
Cigarette burning on the floor next to your ear
Your son is in the driver seat of the truck outside,
        Hank Sr. blaring
        Passenger door open, waiting for you
Your wife has a chicken in her hand
Feathers on her sweater
Blood spots on her boots
Tobacco tucked in her lip
The top stair was loose
Get to it after I pay the bills, you mumbled
Another promise to fulfill
Your workers are in rhythm in your fields
They think about the money they put away for Christmas
They have *novias, esposas, niños, padres, abuelos   Promesas*
They have unlucky friends you refuse to hire
hard working family men you tell them
You refuse to budge even for a *bueno amigo*

Your wife will walk out to the truck
Whisper to your son

Then
She'll rock back on her heels and whistle towards the workers
She pats the truck like a broken horse
Your son takes the bills and cash, closes the passenger door and speeds off
The workers come toward the house
One by one they follow your wife inside stopping only to knock dirt and shit off their boots
They see you on the floor
        Lying still
        Cigarette still burning
Necklaces are pulled from t-shirts and flannels
Crosses are kissed after a chorus of hands touch foreheads, chests, right shoulder then left shoulder
A box of new boots is retrieved from somewhere outside and placed beside you
Each man hugs your wife, kisses her cheek
Then says, *Buen hombre*
Your wife stands in front of the men, speaks demure
Trabajas mañana?
Sammy, the second in charge, steps to the front of the group
Si, mañana
He takes the chicken
The chicken will be returned later by a woman who's buried husbands and sons
She will keep the house clean and the table full until your wife regains the weight she will lose
The workers leave
Your wife squints at the dust clouds
Closes the door before the dust clouds invade the house

19

She sits on the floor beside you
Puts a hand on your chest
Kisses your forehead
Reaches into her sweater and pulls out a phone with her left hand
Pocket pistol with her right hand
She looks at you
She looks at the picture of Jesus above the front door
She looks at the house from the inside
Looks at her hands
Lifts the right one

City by the Sea

Every house looks and smells like a used book store
or antique shop with the scent of coffee and tea
piping through the halls constantly

The rugs naturally blend in with the wooden floor

The doorknobs and locks are new

The windows are portholes due to the harsh storm season

The sun has to sneak in or satisfy itself resting on roofs that hang over the porch

The houses match the old bones that inhabit them

Creaking, bending, breathing with the seasons

Arthritic fingers find relief in warm dishwater or gripping pans for a good foot soak

Sweaters don't get put away and boots are a mainstay

Every porch has a dog that's better off since it was rescued from suburban sewage that puts dogs in sweaters and makes them pose for family photos
These dogs don't need leashes

Just food, water, sleep
And stretches of sand, rock, water and salty air

This place is respite for overworked parents with small children to chase

Grandparents settle in for simple lives that don't require cable or a good steak

Newspapers, yarn, neighbors and salty air

The perfect space for new memories

Grandbabies, tourists, people passing through, boatmen bringing stories, salty air, a new shop downtown

This is the life kid

The harsh winters weed out the unwelcome

This is a postcard

Fireplaces and pebbled driveways

Women with laugh lines and lineage they're ashamed of
Men with coffee stained teeth, stiff shoulders and honest faces that walk the dog to a bar that serves a good breakfast and keeps at least one T.V. on a news channel
Fish scale in the corner

Pictures of dead men next to the tools of their trade
Soldiers with soft eyes full of hope

That's what the tourists come for

They come to rest their elbows at the bar where
their grandfather drank himself to death

They listen for the voices of boatmen, coal miners, and
farmers arguing about who has it rougher and soldiers
leaning on crutches laughing through tears

Some tourists venture upstairs to touch the sheets that
helped grandmothers get their family through hard winters
when men have no work and insatiable appetites

The bartender constantly wipes the photo of his
grandfather and great-uncle

Every hour is happy hour when you've survived this long

The streets have subtle grooves where asphalt was laid over
old wagon tracks

There's a train that doesn't move, but the whistle blows for
kids to get free ice cream in what used to be a sleeper car

The city protects its history and unknowingly becomes an
island where there shouldn't be one

Waking and sleeping with the sun

Gifted with crystals sent from the ocean

City by the sea

Debbie

Another day and time
Your husband would be long gone
Buried in the field next to his parents and sister
You would take care of things
You always could
You know how to keep the boys in line
they listen to you
Mama's boys
Raised hard and heavy handed
Tough like their daddy
    Honest
    Hard working boys
You never cared for the young foolish life
    You were meant to marry
    Meant to have a proud husband and brutish boys
    A hard life
Whatever life earns keep for a woman
Slaughtering pigs and chickens
Stocking the cellar with preserves,
Filling freezers with venison
Cursing your mother for preparing you for a hard life
Your husband died with his boots on,
The boys will do the same
They are too slow for a city girl
Too good for a farm girl
Your boys need mothers who
    Cook
    Sew
    Speak up to forgive
    Work

Mothers who don't fret a broken nail 'cause that's not as bad as dropping a hoe on your ankle,
Your boys need mothers who sleep with their hands on their stretch marks
Mothers with no friends
    There's the house
    The husband
    The boys
    That's enough
Your angel hair never sees daylight
It only touches your face when you shower
Never been poisoned by a beautician
It's your mother's hair
You have your father's backbone
You've spared yourself your mother's regret
You had your boys
    Your men
Your husband saw lack of pride as a sin
    He figured out life in dirty coveralls and
    squinting through cigarette smoke
    New boots and tobacco for Christmas
    If he saw a birthday, that's the gift
    Save your money for the boots
He loved you with precision
You forgave his tendencies and kept your sins in a hope chest
He had to die first
He promised you a long life and boys
You gave him sons and forgiveness
You told the coroner

Leave his boots
Give him a fresh Marlboro and put the pack
in his pocket with his lighter
Don't touch his hair
The boys will bury him

I Lay Dying

It's not easy to stand out amongst the roses when they grow wild
    Can't understand what keeps the soil moist and fertile
I want to stand out amongst the roses in wide open spaces
    My arms and legs are curious
    My mind is an undisturbed planet
    My heart is acid paper
Can I stand out amongst the roses?
    Without name or title
    Breathing well and seeing clear
    My feet secure
    I won't fall into this fertile soil
    I'm strengthened by the sun
    My toes fall in love with each other
I've never stood taller
I am amongst the roses
Infused with the sun as the day turns over and my sight
adjusts to the disappearing day
My heart ages and my toes won't sleep
My mind wants company but my lips won't speak
I smell tenderness around me and for a moment I remind
myself God is beautiful and I am lucky
I stand amongst the roses
Stealing some of their luster but pronouncing my own
Standing tall and bowing with grace not depravity or shame
    I have a name to be spoken
    A scent to be remembered

A life amongst roses in open space my arms and legs attempt
to define but revel in the expanse
       I am child nowhere near my aging skin and
dwindling perception of life
I am amongst the roses
I breathe in so deep they intertwine, overwhelm my senses
and reveal a place for me to rest
My heart shivers, my eyes flicker
I breathe like a child just fed and ready for sleep as I lay dying

Jesus is Homeless

His car breaks down and he walks away
    His wife is skinny with saggy breasts
His kids have black circles around their eyes
    His family goes to the Salvation Army in the winter
They stand in line downtown in the summer
    His wife uses paper towels and toilet paper for pads
    His wife tells everyone the children are homeschooled
    She can read a bus schedule,
Jesus can read cards and count small bills
Jesus works at being poor
    He steals from his jobs, lies
When he is not well, Jesus crams his family into his father's basement
    Jesus blames his mother for everything
His friends are reliable when he has money, but they don't fight for him when there is trouble
Jesus fakes seizures in the winter sometimes and sneaks his family into the hospital room to take blankets, sheets, and a hot shower
Jesus gets his wife pregnant again and he makes her panhandle while he sits across the street in the shade
    Jesus tells social workers he hears voices
He looks like he wouldn't survive county jail – Jesus knows this so he is careful to not break the law
    Jesus loves his family, but doesn't know how to take care of them

The voices are real and don't sleep, so Jesus doesn't sleep
        His wife is always tired and his children are hungry
Jesus looks at them helplessly
        He thinks
My hands are tied and I am weary

War Dogs

Trigger fingers are buried in dust tracks from patrols
And toys turn the tides of war
You are allowed to hate children now
      You can scoff at dolls and such
          You can avoid pregnant women like the plague
You may find yourself putting your life above others
You may have to point a gun at an unruly child
You may have to reach under a dress while a husband
kneels with a bloody mouth and a .45 pointed at his temple

You may have to redefine hero
A ride in the country loses its luster
Sometimes the night sky is clear enough to count
your brothers
Your mother won't stop cooking
Your father says your noise wakes the demons he thought
were gone
Your wife mistakes silence for healing
Your children walk past you one at a time and piggy backs
are a no-no
Many anniversaries and birthdays later you will understand
collateral damage
At least your friends understand
They ask about life overseas
When you are able
You cry when the house is asleep
Otherwise,

Dinner is just as good if it's a little cold and you can take all the time you need to join everyone

We all love you
Remember that

Abridged Kids

Muffin tops and cut-offs
    Shaved heads and beat up skateboards
    Tall cans and paper sacks
Boom boxes spitting old rap music or somebody
screaming murder or mother
Too many people sharing one cigarette
    Tell me there's an artist in the bunch
Someone who can see the mystique in the momentum of a
mosh pit or a break dance circle
Someone who sees the fishnets on a stumpy leg as sexy
and not tragic
Someone who knows that Converse are the only fashion
that crosses all lines
Someone who'll write the stories behind every scar, tattoo,
and broken home
Someone who's tag rivals anything hanging in MOMA
or Paris
Someone who knows why mother and father are the dirty
words to these kids

Dead Hair and Rolling Baskets

The neighborhood changed
    That was my apartment up there
I kept violets in the window
Painted the walls periwinkle
I wore lavender sundresses in the spring
    My husband made a garden in the courtyard
He planted roses for us
    We both worked at the school down the street
I had kindergarten; he was a P.E. teacher
    We drove book mobile in the summer with the kids
They played in a park right there where the gas station is
    We rode the bus to the market on Saturdays
Church over there on Sundays
    My husband died on that bench over there,
I saw him from the window
    He just sat down and leaned over like he was sleeping
Too much running I guess
    We were okay, the kids and I
I got the kids through college
    I kept teaching
Then things changed
    All the good kids moved out
Some kids came back from time to time
    Different
    Loud
Yelling
Fighting

It smelled different around here
        They had loud kids
They didn't take care of themselves, their kids,
or their mothers
        My girlfriends
        1 by 1
        Gone
        Heart attack, stroke,
Myrna got shot by her son
He said she was holding out
What does that mean?
        Holding out
She gave him all her money
        She had to eat with me most days
All these fucked up kids with their fucked up kids
        I don't know what happened
I lost my apartment
        My kids don't come around
My girlfriends are gone
        My husband died
If I take my medicine I can handle it all
        If I don't take my medicine I get real bad cramps
and my skin gets cold
Feels like death coming
Can you help an old lady out?
I don't have enough to get my meds today
God bless you

Raggedy Jan

Raggedy Jan at Cedar and Mur-Len
She got a mother and father
    But don't bother with them
Jan loves Sam
    But Sam gets mad
Cause Jan can get money whenever Sam can't
    She'll kneel, lay or stand if you give money to Jan
Dirty deeds, dirty money
    Dirty needles, little bags
Cause Sam taught Jan to find a vein where she can
    Now Jan always stands at Cedar and Mur-Len

Kansas

Sunsets were made for long drives with silent copilots,
      A few loose strands of hair get tucked behind ears or swept to the side
Bench seats of vinyl, white and sky blue trim
      Feet curled over my dashboard or hanging out the window conducting concertos in 2/2 time
      My right shoulder a head rest
      My arm an arm rest
Maybe the wind will change and my lap will be a foot rest
There's a low hum of a few horses who thought today was perfect day for a stampede across the Kansas prairie
Black shoes on these horses cushion the gallop of travelling lands God didn't think to give a name or populace
      We're not ready to settle
The dust in the air and the pinging of pebbles are currency enough to buy another round for my horses who will drink their fill and head into the wild
      My copilot taps the dashboard and curls into my chest
I grip the harness, urge my horses, and we charge towards the mountains of Colorado

Blackness

I've lived many lives
    Thriving in horrid times
I am the Ripper and the Reaper
A methodical mastermind
    There is no one more dedicated to perfection
Without me
There is chaos
    Sloppy living and constant pain
Someone has to tear off the band-aid
Cradle the body while the band plays
Bring purpose to the light of day and stigma to dark hallways
    I am a genius perfecting child's play
I am the worker who neither rests nor strays

The Chosen

Murder's in the air tonight baby
        And I'm feeling good
My nose smells power
        My lungs take in the mayhem
I exhale order
And become king

The Kennel

Tonight there'll be smear marks on table tops
counters and windows
There'll be blood and shit on shafts and sheets
Claw marks on necks and backs, swollen sockets, puffy
cheeks, and broken teeth
Tonight's not safe for silicone, collagen, botox or weaves
There'll be no room for timidity
There'll be cause for confessions and PERK kits
There'll be rumors and suspicion
There'll be apologies, long showers and not enough blame
to go around
       There'll be manhunts, APBs, anonymous tips,
and ER visits
There'll be no room for cries, heroes, or hesitation
       There'll be cause for home security, executions,
and a clear memory
Tonight
I let myself out of the cage

What We Do When No One's Watching

When no one's watching
    We thank God he invented revenge
    Shovels become hammers, hatchets and fists
    We wipe sweat with the back of our hand
    or a rag from the trunk
When no one's watching
    The tree is a mausoleum
    The roots are the catacombs
    Black plastic caskets for my enemies
When no one's watching
    Cars become courtrooms and motels
    Children become judge and jury
    Girlfriends become wives and wives
    become lawyers and psychologists
When no one's watching
    Apologies are a waste of time
    Forgiveness is a waste of time
    Who to pin the truth on is all that matters
When no one's watching
    My thoughts have no beginning or end
    They want to get out, but my hands are
    holding them in
When no one's watching
    I am a genius
    I am nobody's victim
    I am in control
The voices told me so

Wayco

I don't need violence to give power to the poem
But when debts aren't paid
The noise in my head doesn't stop until
      My arm lifts
      Stiffens
I exhale a count to five to slow down my heart
I pause
      My forearm twitches 3 times
I inhale through my nose and walk away
Lowering my arm until it rests at my side
Relaxed
Dangling
I ease back into the shadows
Remove the gloves and mask
Start a small fire behind an empty house
And return to my original plans

Maestro

My hands need a guitar or harp
to bring melody to the madness of my drumming
heart

Above All Else

The watchful eye
Sees every side
      Hears nary truth
Sees every lie

ABCs of Life

Always be curious
Don't ever fight grace
Harness intelligence justice kindness
Leave manipulation negativity out
Precise query
Run
Sleep
Teach universally
Violence wins X
Youthful zest!

Flint Am I

A presumed wasteland
        And questionable tactics
More feeble answers

Dress Shopping

Nobody likes a fat girl darling
        Lazy neither
                And oh lord!
Don't be stupid
You will never see a man OR woman unless you paying
for something
        And I mean that in every way you can imagine

Now me,
        I dress to kill,
        Smile pretty,
        And I got more information in my head than the
CIA, NSA,
        and FBI all put together,
Think anybody ever call me fat, lazy, or stupid?
        I wouldn't know
My mother named me Lizzie Ann

Now
Let me see that smile

What We Deserve

There are so many women around with nothing on
their mind
        They are dressed and out with their man
Thinking is done unless she hasn't mastered walking
and laughing on cue
        If he does everything he usually does
She doesn't have to think
        His clothes are in the ballpark of every other day
        He talks like he always has
        His hands are familiar
        Even his hair is the same
        He is a mirror to yesterday
        He doesn't open the door
He never has
        He ignores her pleas to let her talk
Same
        He grips her hand too tight
Same
        He looks at every woman the same way he looks at her
She knows
She pushes her hair away from her face
Makes a vague attempt to speak, but laughs because
she knows what's coming
        She laughed at the wrong time
        She has to think now
She never knew her man didn't like to be laughed at

Haircuts and Cold Drinks

Dad, what do I do?
I like this girl
>Son,
>I don't know too much about women,
>All I can tell is what I learned from being
>with your mother,

What's that?
>Kiss the girl,
>Tell her she's beautiful and kiss her again,
>Then keep kissing her,

That's it?
>Kiss the girl,
>Tell her she's beautiful and kiss her again,
>Then keep kissing her

When do I stop?
>I haven't

The Village

      A mother's work is never done
Not when there's absentee fathers, over-time, and homework
      A father's work is never done
Because nothing overpowers his good intentions and honest efforts
      A grandmother's work is never done
Not with them all around and pots on the stove
      A grandfather's work is never done
He's not some strutting bank roll
He just loves them all
But they don't know he can't feel his toes when he walks
      An auntie's work is never done
Cause that was her sister
And she made a promise
      An uncle's work is never done
Because the parents are too scared to tell the truth, but it must be said
      A cousin's work is never done
'Cause they grew up together
And that's just family
      A sister's work is never done
Not because she wants to
Because she has to
      A brother's work is never done
Not because he wants to
Not because he has to

Because he knows they need him
        The baby's work is never done
To remind them all of why they're here

Issue

What do you mean the room isn't ready?
How long?
Really?
Honey, we have to wait. Room isn't ready
Can you believe it?
$1200 dollars a night and the room isn't ready
I'm paying for the room to be ready
Come on hun, we can wait in the lobby
You want something from the bar? I'm getting a headache.
  Car service was late
  Now, I got to wait for a room I paid for in advance
I'm calm
I'm just upset
I don't deserve this
  I work hard
  I pay taxes
  I deserve to be treated with some respect
I'll be right back
I got our drinks
What are they talking about on the news?
Hey, look at this
More kids dying from starvation in…
How do you pronounce that?
  Cy-ree, Sear ree uh
Wow, somebody should do something
I know. I know. It's tragic. But hey, that's the world we live in
Oh, here's our guy

The room must be ready
Leave the bags, hun
Someone will take care of them
After what they put us through, we deserve to be taken
care of for a while
Hey guy, I'm sorry I don't know your name. Can you bring
up some fresh drinks to our room after you get the bags?

If We Are Loving

If we are loving
We negate the language of hate
We disembowel ourselves of reasons for dissolution
If we are loving
    We embrace synthesis
    We are in concert with others
Every conversation begins with you, I speak of myself last
If we are loving
    We eliminate the percentages
    We take down mirrors and walls
If we are loving
    Apologies become obsolete
    Power measures the output of effort for the greater good
If we are loving
    Life is luxurious
    Each moment is lavish
If we are loving
    Death is a well received promise
    We marvel at what will come and what we left behind

Work

Art happens away from life
    How can I explain to Sharon, that I hear footsteps
and heartbeats?
I smell the stench of urine seeping through hot tar,
I smell the residue of breast milk on sore nipples cloaked by
cigarette smoke
My mind is alive
    My pen pirouettes in my palm,
I'm a tourist at home
    Backpacking the same streets,
Bathing in fountain mist
    Thank God for rain and kind strangers,
Thank God for soft grass under the shade trees along Paseo
    Art is happening and life becomes a menagerie
as my pen twirls
My mind is alive and growing tentacles
    Touching every women I molest mentally
Strangling every man I confront in the Crossroads
    Torturing every foul mouthed child
Commanding everyone to turn away from the crimes I
commit
Returning stray bullets to the shooter for a second chance
Catching good people at the moment they go rogue
Flicking on the lights at the right time
Disturbing the peace of abuse
The tentacles do their work
Retract back into my mind
I convulse
And the pen curtsies

Dumpster Diving

Somewhere amongst the throw a ways has to be something of value

Strange Hands That Pray

We are in preparation and showing diligence to the task of asking masking nothing; Humming and singing in unison uniting us in need; we are greedy for touches with oil and splashes of water to avoid gnashing of teeth;
We are speaking in a code known to those within these houses; these mansions women and men stand in with the intention of causing explosions and excitement

A delirium meant to drive away the demons and convert the wicked

Sermon

We're sanctified and electrified
WiFi without limitation
      Gracious without hesitation
Love without hatred
      We are in the spirit of the giving season
We are
Tired
Hungry
And thirsty
But we don't want
Rest
Food
Or water
We want saving
Peace
And forgiveness
We need
Honor
Truth
And love
We desire lives that are honest and dependable
We strive for perfection
We admire the effort
We understand falling but don't accept falling away
We ask God for guidance
So when we kneel
Fall

Stumble
Or drop to our knees
Our humbleness is a sign of what is required along with
the work of faith
There is no one walking strong enough to take away
our power
I am lifted with my head down
Palms up to receive the blessings
To God be the glory!

Penthouse

I wish you knew me better
I wish I didn't have to leave notes around the apartment about what's wrong and what I meant to say
I wish I could talk to you when you're awake
Touch you when you're not lying down and facing away from me
I wish I knew how to catch you before you fall back onto the bed
      You talk to me over your shoulder
You wake up and leave so quickly
      You mumble my name like you don't know me
But, you put your cheek on my shoulder when I'm reading
      You invade my space with childish curiosity
I just want to be in your dreams
      So I breathe on your neck when you're sleeping
And I brush your calves with the top of my feet to hear you moan and say stop
      I offer my arm as a bony pillow so you'll touch me roughly
I invade your space with my body to somehow put me in your dreams
      Maybe then you'll be forced to turn around when you talk to me
Or speak my name out loud like you own me
      But keep putting your cheek on my shoulder when I read
I like to believe that for a time we are thinking the same things

No One

I was waiting and no one came
I wasn't sure, but I left anyway and walked and talked about
things people talk about when no one's around
I walked somewhere, I can't remember
      No one was around is all I know
And I shared some things about going nowhere and what it
means to be tired and not wanting to wait and no one shows
up and the day happens anyway
I was afraid of you not coming around or some other thing
I can't describe – and no one came
And I fell in love anyway on a day of walking somewhere and
talking about some things and doing it all with no one
      So,
What I'm saying is,
      Stay where you are
And I hope you find no one to walk beside
Talk to
And fall in love with

Parking Lots

Shayla's at home
> And I don't see why going there changes anything

Lou Ann is always so easy going and laughs at my jokes.
> Shayla just grunts and smokes

I don't want to leave home
I just want to play house with another baby doll

Hospice

Will we have moments to make memories
      Or will time lie to us again about possibilities
Will we realign our sins and pray together
      Will we find another source of heat and burn
without need of oxygen
Will we leave paw prints and teeth marks on each other
      Will we have the energy for running and catching up
Will we trade imagination for harsh realities
Will we let the castle crumble from the inside and rebuild
on soft sands contoured by light breezes
Or will you once again don a hard hat and tool belt with
our plans in your grasp
Will we silence ourselves entreaty for peace or become litigants
      How will we eat when our hunger erupts
      Will there be a table for two or buffets with paper
plates and plastic ware
Will we count our blessings or tally marks
      Will we still be insatiable or appeased by boundaries
Will our hopes parallel a ray of light or the letter Z
      Will we trespass without worry of guard dogs or
barbed wire
Will there be open doors or signs warding off solicitors
      Will our shadows reveal our secrets or are they still in
the dark
Will we talk our way through tempests
      Or has something invaded the conversation
Will we be us?

Gray Matter

Your children's children are your parents
You feel like a baby sitter and find yourself telling stories of when you were young
You have to cut food into small pieces and meal times are challenging
There are accidents to clean up and impromptu games of hide-and-seek
You sleep when they sleep and they barely sleep a wink
Friends and family have good intentions, but reach their limit in about a week
Tomorrow is far away
        You deal with day-to-day
They say I love you
        Cause that's what you say

Night Run

I breathe in cold air
and am reminded
that I am one of a few
who see the pain of life
as an invitation to greatness

175th

I bike towards South Johnson County
I heard it looks like Kenya when you get past the houses
There are open fields and you can feel the sun from every angle
        The ground is hard and dry
For now I see manicured lawns, SUV's and delivery trucks
Am I alone wondering what Africa looks like and smells like
I see Texas in everything
My mother's life and stories can only take me where her hearts been
        In her father's house
        In school liking a boy
        Staying away from the crowds of fast girls
        Raising a family with my father, a Texas boy himself
        Far from the Africa
But I've lived Texas through my mother
My life is too nomadic
In a fog of imagination

I make it past the houses to open fields
I park my bike and sit down with my back to the road
I sit thinking about Texas and wondering if this side of Kansas is Africa
        It's all Kenya
I am told this by a girl with long black hair, curling toes and unwrinkled skin
She was walking
Saw me and my bike

And now asks where I'm from
I point south thinking of my mother and father
I ask her
She points east and pulls back her hair
We both wonder what brought us here
She sits next to me and tells me to take my shoes and socks
off and walk in the grass
    Repeat the songs she sings
    Imagine goat and ugali cooking
    Picture nappy headed children with white
    teeth chasing each other around me
She asks if I've had chai
opens a steaming bottle
and pulls 2 cups from her bag
I smell the chai, but I also smell the goat cooking
I look around for a fire and see smoke in the distance
I hear footfalls and giggles all around me
    I tell the girl to think about stories she's heard from
her mother
    I ask her if her father is honest
    And does she have precocious sisters
    That's my Texas I tell her and drink my chai
She says she is here because she needed a break from home,
but likes the memory
I tell her the same and take a last sip of my chai
    My hands are in my lap and my cup is empty
    My legs are relaxing
The girl lets her hair down, ruffles it and refills my cup
The sun sets and we inhale in unison
It's good to go home every once in a while

B.P.s

Black people aren't poetic because of Afru-ika, the West Indies, the Jacobins, the Carribean, middle passages, European dissent, drums, voices, hair, noses, Crow, Equiano, Sojourner, Scott, Allen, Garvey, Coltrane, Baldwin, DeLaney, Billie, Fats, Obama, Mississippi, Georgia, Louisiana, Arkansas, Indiana, Harlem, Watts, LA, Chicago, Detroit, Muhammed, Clarence X
Our parents
Our grandparents
Family reunions
Jumping brooms
Weddings in living rooms
Unmarked graves where Henrietta Lacks looms
You know what
Forget what I said before
This shit is poetic

Escape Route

Escape must sound like the flutter flapping of birds
wings since we are trying to rise above the wrongs
here on the ground

Escape can't sound like waves slapping against the sides of
dinghys
Or the choking and coughing of fathers and mothers
splashing and kicking with babies on their backs

Escape can't sound like grunts and shushing and
panting and footfalls in the jungle – machetes and
arms and hands pushing and hacking through webs
of vines and brush

Escape can't sound like helicopters whirring, stirring
dust that pelts tired faces and battered villages

Escape can't sound like pebbles and rocks rolling
beneath clumsy feet struggling to trek down
mountains and hillsides

Escape is not the clopping of livestock that will keep
us from starving or provide currency for shelter

Escape can't be grinding gears and dying engines,
fists pounding the dashboard, doors slamming,
groans of indecision to fight or run

Escape can't sound like hushed voices around crackling fires,
The sweeping sound of cold hands rubbing together
The click of weapons preparing for battle
Does escape sound like single shots from heirloom pistols and rifles that are used for hunting and scaring predators, but now must fight

Is escape water sloshing in jugs, bare feet clamoring up ladders and ankles snapping on impact on the other side of the wall

Does escape sound like last rites in low tones to those that are left

Is escape flies buzzing around the carcusses of friends, loved ones and neighbors

Does escape sound like splashes in the ocean from bodies avoiding an impending fate

No

Escape must sound like the flutter and flapping of birds wings since we are trying to rise above the wrongs here on the ground

Inner Peace

I don't turn my back on suffering
I brace myself for the impact when the SUV jumps 4
lanes and a family is torn apart
I fine tune my vision so I can see the drywall explode
as the bullet searches for a victim
I sit in emergency rooms and watch as lies become reasons
I lay in battlefields yelling *stop* in every direction

I don't turn my back on suffering, but I don't know
how to run to its side and talk it through the pain
I can't stop the car or the bullet or the lies or the battles
But I can ask God to teach me his name in Hindu,
Arabic, Hebrew and every other language more
beautiful than my native tongue

I can bow my head when I say *hello* or *thank you* to anyone
I can be humble and not be quiet
I can turn and turn back and back again
      Spinning
If I spin fast enough with my hands open maybe
my momentum will save a family
return a bullet to its owner
reverse the lies and stop the battle

But, I think I need to say God's name in another language
What's more humbling, unquiet
True
And a reason to spin with my hands open

Letter to 1985 from 2012

The sleeping mountain wakes and the line of tension breaks
making black eyes on my baby doll
Satchels spreading sickness
A bomb handling police business
Ignoring there's children
trapped because of the house's position
putting black eyes on my baby doll
3rd degree burns, screams can't protect you at all
       Just leaves black eyes on my baby doll
Paralyzed from the waist down
No safety in your own town
Beat the boy from the third floor
       Putting black eyes on my baby doll
Can't move fast enough
Too tired and hurt to pull yourself up
You feel like you're dying
Keep getting beat up
       My baby doll's eyes are black, face puffed
Opposite sides
Neither will survive 85
       Black balls for my baby doll's eyes
Shots and lies
We're flooded from the inside
11 died, just 1 provides reasons to cry
       With white fingers and black baby doll eyes

I'm reaching to build bridges from
John Africa to Omayra Sanchez
      Black baby doll eyes and
Money serves no penance
9 can speak, but have yet to finish a sentence
One speaks and her mother won't hear it
She's clearly talking to my spirit
Neck deep in waters I had just discovered

Had we met that summer
I would have told them to kick like Ms. Julie says
If your arms get tired and you don't want to drown

Mare Internum

The crown is losing shape and luster
Jammed and stuffed in boats off the Lybian coast
Once again black bodies head north for solace
    Fleeing
    Starving
    Beaten
    Raped
    Dying
    Singing
    Praying
One upon another
    Scared
    Powerless
    Hopeful
    Starving
    Dying
    Singing
    Praying
The sky is quiet
The boat is wet on the inside
It's not just babies who cry
Mothers and fathers have prayed enough to walk to Sicily
The men just want to work and take care of their families
They are farmers and tradesmen even in a world of stock prices and voice activated devices

The women want to feed, but feeble boats keep the baby from latching
And mothers die with one breast rolling like the waves
    God save Africa
    But what of Africans
Once again white faces appear in boats

My World

There better be black boys in heaven
We've given the world too many gifts to just die in shit
    I know you want names, but I can't see their faces
    Some were ornamentation
    Or a pool of blood dotted with shell casings
Twisted limbs on the ground
An expected dismount for gymnasts who spend their life
running and flipping without coaches or safety nets
Or did God cut the strings on his puppets just as they asked
to be real boys
    I know you want names
But even when we talk I'm checking for signs of life
    Voices
    Chests heaving
    Pupils dilating and narrowing
    Shoulders and elbows flexed as we clasp hands and
    part ways
I want to hear their names, know their life
But I smell death on them and wonder if I emit the same odor

An old voice keeps me out of the woods
Away from grass and flowers decorated with remnants of
twine and an unidentified feather held in place by droplets of tar
The air is polluted with the scent of liquor and gasoline
There is a burnt outline of a body on the side of a tree
Red marks on the roots
Somewhere else there's snow on the ground, a smoking gun,

voices crackling on a police radio, a toy gun loosely gripped by my 12 year old self
Black boys are in my memories from times and places I've never lived
We share nothing but skin
    God won't let us die as old men with families
He constantly decides that somehow we deserve lesser
So we don't waste time crying or talking
We beg in silence for a life valued by anyone breathing the same air
We are deprived of the arena gladiators fought where they were at least given the façade of honor
My father and grandfather managed to survive wars thousands of miles from their home
    The store is less than a mile from my home
    Will I make it?
I fear no man
I fear for him
As long as God is making the decisions
    But he owes us
He owes black boys a place in heaven
Somewhere that's just as safe as our grandfather's truck,
    Our grandmother's kitchen
    Our mother's arms
    Our father's hands
    Our own dreams
He owes us

Olathe Riders

Bury my heart in Kansas,
If that is home,
Until then,
I chase the fire of sunset,
Riders at my side astride Appaloosas and Mustangs,
Our minds drift between finding home and small game for quick meals to reenergize our travels,
I'm comforted by the riders at my side,
Bred warriors,
Smart enough to know when war is necessary,
One of them an elder with the skin of surviving many battles,
Together we chase the flame of sunset,
    Looking for home,
Getting stronger with each gallop of hoofs that rattle the earth and pronounce our charge,
My riders don't see the Kansas Gordon Parks will fall in love with,
    They don't see passage to anywhere
    They smell the bodies beneath the prairie grass
    They see the flame of Kansas sky in the horizon
    They ask if we are getting closer to the God they heard about
They see the ash of darkening sky smoldering the fire and say Olathe in unison
    They ask if we are home
I say we should go South to find others, find more of our own
    The elder grunts
    Points West

      He urges his horse and forces us to follow,
      He kicks and leans forward
The horse digs its hoofs deep into the sand and rock and
prairie grass fusing its body with the elder's becoming
a comet
Their hairs are contrails
      The elder's skin tightens and he is younger than I
and the other riders
      He reverses time with determination,
The other riders and I age with the desperation of chasing
The elder and his horse could walk across galaxies
touching every star while the other riders and I struggle to
keep pace
Our trotting horses fight us,
Refusing to gallop side by side with the elder willing to
settle in this desolate terrain
We beg
Kicking and urging
Our horses gallop with restraint
Their heads high
Acknowledging the fear of the other riders and I
At last the elder pulls on the reins
Settles onto his horse and nods
The flame of the horizon extinguished by the weight of
ash and leaves a white hole in the black sky
I look out and see milk poured onto the water
Our destination
Our true course
The calm of Hillsdale Lake
Home

One Love

It was summer
Someone discovered Bob Marley and we decided we were
going to live on our feet
Running
      We thought we could outrun what our parents were
afraid of
We thought we could love our way through anything even
our tangled view of the world
We saw the tanks at Tienaman square
We felt the heat of napalm burning the clothes of Kim Phuc
We smelled the burning flesh of the Thich Quang Duc,
Michael Schwarner, Andre Goodman, James Chaney, Addie
Mae, Cynthia Wesley, Carole Roberson, Denise Miller
We screamed for Asifa, Baby P, Victoria, Leiliana, Baby
Brianna, Shamiya
We'd heard about Adam, Emmit, Alan, Precious Doe, Jessica
and Hector and knew community still existed
The world stops for children
      So we became them
Falling back on the ground and watching bullets fly overhead
Wishing Amado, Gregory and Michael could be down here
with us among the living and the loving
      We hear One Love once and put the song on repeat
Lying on the ground wondering if the song can be heard
overseas
      We think about God for a second, but the clouds give
us clearer answers

We see the storms brewing and moving toward us, then
away to unsuspecting victims
    We turn the music up louder
The bullets stop flying, but the images stay
So we get up and dance hard until our heels are calloused
and the earth cracks
    We dance harder and our sweat seeps into the ground
We turn the music up louder
Dance harder
Those two words don't belong together
ONE LOVE
Our hips hurt and our hair is getting longer
The earth is opening up
    We dance harder
    We ask ourselves how we can share this feeling with
the world
    And we turn the music up
    We see more faces
    We call their names into the ether
Jessica and Kelli Uhl, Terrell Peterson, Hector Pieterson,
Nixzmary Brown, Liam Fee, Imette Carnella, Jennifer Moore,
Mbuyisa Makhubu
    We keep their names alive for their families
    We dance hard
    We turn the music up louder for the world
ONE LOVE

Paradise

We vacation in places people are facing starvation
Middle passage paradise
Staycations for
        Jamaicans
        Haitians
        Dominicans
        And West Indians
So far removed we can't say brother or sister unless the
DJ plays it
If we're as close as we think
We wouldn't bypass poverty to be served food and drink
        Or let marijuana leaf unify our experience and
mystique
Our distant relatives are dangerous and poor
        Poverty is an eye sore
American blacks become benefactors to their troubled past
We suddenly want to read and know everyone around us
Do things we don't usually do
        Relax every muscle
        Smile at the morning
        Think about home
        Look at the water
The men fishing
Children working and playing at the same time
Women cooking and making beds
Our feet elevated.

Tank Tops and Collarbones

    Mouthing words and acknowledging my stare
    Criss-crossing your feet
    Adjusting in your seat
    Scooping and flipping your hair or
    pushing it behind your ear –
You want to come home with me
You want to peel off that tank top and let me figure out where you spray perfume
You want to walk out of your shorts and panties and shoes and socks
    I'd follow your trail to the moon
You want orgasms to come with confetti and balloons
Let me drown you in celebration
    My bathroom is a lagoon in Iceland
    My bedroom is Montecristo
    My couch is an island in the Philippines
    My kitchen is a ferry in San Francisco bay
    Every hallway and doorway is a landing strip
My penis is G6

Waco Porter is the author of *Total Eclipse*, a collection of poetry. He lives in Kansas City with his wife and three girls. He loves to swim, bike and run when he's not writing or reading.

www.ingramcontent.com/pod-product-compliance
Lightning Source LLC
Chambersburg PA
CBHW022014120526
44592CB00034B/811